What Did Jesus Say When They Asked Him How to Pray?

I0833714

What Did Jesus Say When They Asked Him How to Pray?

The Words and the History of the Lord's Prayer

BY John Ohst

RESOURCE *Publications* • Eugene, Oregon

WHAT DID JESUS SAY WHEN THEY ASKED HIM HOW TO PRAY?
The Words and the History of the Lord's Prayer

Copyright © 2026 John Ohst. All rights reserved. Except for brief quotations in critical publications or reviews, no part of this book may be reproduced in any manner without prior written permission from the publisher. Write: Permissions, Wipf and Stock Publishers, 199 W. 8th Ave., Suite 3, Eugene, OR 97401.

Resource Publications
An Imprint of Wipf and Stock Publishers
199 W. 8th Ave., Suite 3
Eugene, OR 97401

www.wipfandstock.com

PAPERBACK ISBN: 979-8-3852-7366-9
HARDCOVER ISBN: 979-8-3852-7367-6
EBOOK ISBN: 979-8-3852-7368-3

VERSION NUMBER 04/07/26

Scripture quotations marked New RSV are from the New Revised Standard Version Bible, copyright © 1989 National Council of the Churches of Christ in the United States of America. Used by permission. All rights reserved worldwide.

Quotations marked RSV are from the Revised Standard Version of the Bible, copyright © 1946, 1952, and 1971 the Division of Christian Education of the National Council of the Churches of Christ in the United States of America. Used by permission. All rights reserved.

Quotations from the Good News Bible are from the Good News Translation® (Today's English Version, Second Edition) Copyright © 1992 American Bible Society. All rights reserved.

Quotations from the Contemporary English Version are from the Contemporary English Version® Copyright © 1995 American Bible Society. All rights reserved.

This book is dedicated to

God

for all the blessings we have been given.

In Appreciation
From the Author, John Ohst

I would like to thank
the entire staff of Wipf and Stock
for all the good help they have given me
in preparing my books for publication,
especially the Managing Editor,
the Editorial Administrative Assistant,
the Copy Editors, and the Typesetters.
Your hard work, patience, expertise, and kindness
have meant a great deal to me.
God bless you all.

Contents

Preface

IN THE PAST 2000 years, there have been several manuscripts written about The Lord's Prayer (TLP). Moreover, just in the past fifty years, there have been *hundreds* of books on it, and no two of them are the same. Authors all have their own focus, style, and special viewpoint that they want to emphasize.

Some of them use real-life examples to tell us how TLP can enable us to help the lives of others and our own lives. Some writers demonstrate how Jesus was such a good teacher, preacher, and pastor—not just to his disciples, but to us as well. Sometimes authors use several Bible passages to show their readers how TLP can help them better understand God's purposes, methods, and messages. Occasionally, a writer will use TLP to make us aware of how the physical world that God has created contains so many sources of beauty, wonder, and joy . . . heaven on earth. Some other writers teach us how TLP can lead us into deep insights about ourselves through patient reflection. An author can also emphasize the importance of our spiritual responsibility to pray TLP more frequently and with stronger sincerity.

My purpose in writing about The Lord's Prayer was to closely examine its words and phrases, and to research information on its history, from when it began in the first century up to the ways it is used now in the twenty-first century.

Part 1

The Words of the Lord's Prayer

THE LORD'S PRAYER (ALSO known as the "Our Father," or "Paternoster") is the best known of all the prayers in the Bible. As far as we know, it is the only prayer that Jesus taught us, and it is used today by billions of people. It encompasses all of our basic needs and concerns. And it does it with only about fifty words.

In The Lord's Prayer, there are two main points of focus. In the first part, the focus is on *God*, as can be seen by the first phrase, "Our Father who art in heaven," and by the pronouns (in *italics*) that refer to God:

> Our Father who art in heaven,
> hallowed be *thy* name
> *Thy* kingdom come, *thy* will be done
> on earth as it is in heaven.

The second point of focus is on us, the *people*, and on our daily concerns.

> Give *us* this day *our* daily bread,
> and forgive *us our* trespasses,
> as *we* forgive those who trespass against *us*.
> Lead *us* not into temptation, but deliver *us* from evil.

For those using more words as a conclusion to the prayer (see Part 3, Doxology), the focus returns to *God* and on the eternal greatness of God.

For *thine* is the kingdom
and the power
and the glory,
for ever and ever. Amen

Now, let's take a closer look at some of the words in The Lord's Prayer. It has been said that the very first word is one of the most important words in the entire prayer:

OUR God is not just my God, and not just your God.

God is our God. Moreover, this pronoun "our" is all-inclusive:

God is God of everyone.

God is God of my church and your church.

God is God of Protestant churches and Catholic churches (both Roman and Eastern Orthodox).

God is God of all Christian denominations.

God is God of rational humanistic and metaphysical beliefs, (see Appendix 1, Part B) such as the Unitarian-Universalist and Christian Science.

God is God of all the world's religions, such as Buddhism, Hinduism, Judaism, Taoism, and Islam.

God is God of many ancient traditional faiths, practiced by the aboriginals in North and South America, Europe, Africa, Asia, Australia, and the Pacific Islands.

God is God of non-believers, of agnostics and atheists.

God is God of all living things, of all animals and all plants.

> God is God of all creation, of the air, the land, and the water on earth, and of all the objects in the rest of the universe.
>
> God is *our* God.

FATHER—This noun is one of the most common names for God used by Christians, no doubt because the word "father" has a number of denotations of *what* a father is (parent, patriarch, progenitor), but more importantly for the many connotations of *who* a father is:

Creator: God made all creatures in existence, but not as an impersonal "clockmaker" who wound up the universe when time began and then just moved back to watch. Instead, God has a close, personal, caring, and loving relationship with each one of us. As the Amish say, "God is closer to us than our own breath." (For more on God as Creator, see Appendix 1.)

Provivider: God is also the giver of the mental, physical, emotional, and spiritual strengths that we need each day. Yes, we can also depend on people to give us these things, but people are limited. They cannot always be there when we need them. They have a finite amount of time, wisdom, and power. God's wisdom and power are infinite, everlasting and ever-present.

Protector: God protects us from the negative effects of mental, physical, emotion, and spiritual harm and danger.

Teacher: (one meaning of "rabbi") God teaches us how best to deal with the world, to treat its environment, other creatures, other people, and ourselves. God teaches us how to live—how to think, speak, and act in the best possible ways. He teaches us how to teach ourselves, to pay attention to the world and to the words and ways of life, and to choose the best of them to make all of us better. God teaches us to do the things that are right and good.

Guide: When we're confused as to which way to go, or think, or react, God can show us the way. The problems, of course, are that we don't always ask for this kind of help, or when it does come, we don't always recognize it, or like it, or agree with it, or follow it.

Comforter: During periods of sadness, despair, fatigue, or pain, it's really wonderful to feel the warm presence of God's love right next to us.

Friend: Someone to share our lives with, someone to talk to, for any reason, about good things or bad, in serious discussions or casual conversations, even someone to joke around with! God has an excellent sense of humor and can help us see the humor where none seems to exist.

Listener: God can *always* pay attention to anyone, at any time, at any place, to anything we wish to say on any topic, for any reason.

Savior: We can sometimes find someone to save us from our difficulties, but the one who can best save us from the troublesome times that come to us (or that we bring to ourselves and to others) is God. When no other helping hand is available, God's hand is there, bringing salvation, mercy, forgiveness, redemption, restoration, and love.

WHO ART IN HEAVEN—Heaven can be understood as a spiritual realm of perfection: the source of perfect love, perfect peace, perfect wisdom, and perfect power. Heaven is the source of all that is good and right and true. And being spiritual, heaven is not in any specific physical location, not "beyond the sky" or "high above the earth and sea." If it's anywhere, it's everywhere. Nor is heaven located in any specific time. If it's in any time, it's eternal.

Actually, the "when" of heaven is more important than the "where." It's when a parent or teacher is speaking kind words to a child . . . when a hospital nurse or visitor puts a hand on the shoulder of a patient . . . when you see the aerial ballet of birds wafting their wings in the summer air, or a blue dragonfly resting atop a yellow wildflower. It's when you notice the dark green foliage around a pond, in the woods, along a street, or in a backyard . . . when you feel the loving warmth of a family member, or friend, or furry pet sitting beside you . . . or when your face meets the mist from a white waterfall in front of you. These are but a few examples of how God's kingdom comes and God's will is being done "on earth as it is in heaven."

HALLOWED BE THY NAME—The term "hallowed" comes from an Old English word for "holy." It also gave us the word "Halloween," ("Holy Evening" on the day before "All Saints' Day.")

Even God's name is sacred . . . no matter what name we use. To name a few: Father, Christ, Jesus, Holy Spirit, Yahweh, The Great Spirit, The Great Mystery, Light, Truth, The Almighty, The Word, Master, as well as Lord—a name used thousands of times in the Bible (and expressed as Adonai in Hebrew, or Kyrios in Greek), or simply the name God (in Hebrew: Elohim, in Aramaic: Eli (or Alaha), and in Arabic: Allah.) World-wide, there are well over a thousand names for God. (For more on names, see Appendix 2.)

THY KINGDOM COME—There are so many earthly kingdoms and countries, powers and principalities, each of them having a mix of good and bad qualities. However, what we need and pray for here is that we be ruled first and foremost by God, the divine source of perfect justice, perfect fairness, perfect goodness, and perfect peace.

THY WILL BE DONE—Usually, we want *our* will to be done, and our will may be good, reasonable, even laudable, such as praying for peace and love among people, for relief from bad weather or from physical or mental pain. But our will may also be tainted with self-centeredness and temporal pleasures; so, we may pray for a new job, a new house, a new car, a new spouse or—as some kids still do—pray for a pony! Jesus in Gethsemane was praying for his cup of suffering to pass away. "Yet, not my will but thy will be done." [Mt. 26.39]. Jesus knew God's will is pre-eminent and all-inclusive, centered on all beings, intended for *permanent* goodness and peace, to be given fairly to all God's creatures.

ON EARTH AS IT IS IN HEAVEN—Here we pray that both the kingdom and the will of God become fully manifested here in our world just as they exist in heaven. It may seem frustrating that we must pray for this constantly, but since Jesus intended for us to hope for this by teaching us this prayer, then—whether or not this kind of perfection can be recognized—we should daily keep it as our goal to search for it and to work with God to make it become evident on earth. (For more on heaven and earth, see Appendix 3.)

GIVE US THIS DAY OUR DAILY BREAD—Each day of our lives we need the nourishment of God. Our "daily bread" comes in many forms: the foods we eat and drink, clean air, the physical exercise that strengthens us, the help we receive from family, friends, and others. All things good and necessary that God provides to sustain our bodies and souls.

Martin Luther said much the same (and then some) about 500 years ago when explaining this petitions in the Lord's Prayer: "Daily bread includes everything needed in this life, such as food and clothing, home and property, work and income, a devoted family, an orderly community, good government, favorable weather, peace and health, a good name, and true friends and neighbors." [From *The Small Catechism*, 1529]

It could be said that our "bread" also includes our *intangible* daily needs: kindness, patience, optimism, a sense of humor, the joy of a job well done, the restful peace at the end of the day. Actually, the Greek word for "daily," επιούσιος (a word used in the Greek NT *only* in The Lord's Prayer) can mean not only "needed" or "substantial," but also "super-substantial," *above* material substance. It has been suggested [in *aramaicnt.org*] that επιούσιος was coined by the translator to express the transcendental connotation of the Aramaic word /çorak/.

The fact that we are praying to be given only *today's* bread is God's way of teaching us to take one day at a time. As Jesus said, "So do not be worried about tomorrow, for tomorrow will bring worries of its own. Today's trouble is enough for today." (Mt. 6.34). Actually, the original Greek word for "to be worried" in this passage, μεριμνήσητε, literally means "to let your mind be divided."

Moreover, this mention of "our *daily* bread" testifies to the idea that the entire Lord's Prayer is intended to be used each day, a daily devotion, to center our mind on the things that are really important.

A common way to give thanks for God's daily blessings is to say grace at mealtime. In the words of my German-American grandparents: "Komm, Herr Jesu, sei unser Gast; und segne, was du uns bescheret hast. Amen." My mom and dad used Early Modern English words: "Come, Lord Jesus, be our guest. Let everything thou givest us be blest. Amen."

AND FORGIVE US OUR TRESPASSES—"Trespasses" has a number of synonyms: wrongs, wrongdoings, guilts, sins, evils, transgressions, misbehaviors, misdeeds, mistreatments, or mistakes, including any actions, words, or thoughts which have done harm to others, to ourselves, or to our environment. These errors may be as minor as an unkind word or as major as taking a life. We need to recognize what we have done wrong and admit our guilt to ourselves and to God.

But we should also realize that no matter what we have done, there is always one who will forgive us: God. If we're fortunate, there may be some people in our life who love us enough to forgive us, but that's not always the case. God's love, however, is always there.

God's forgiveness does not erase the wrongdoings; these events are part of our personal history, and once they have happened, they have happened. But the loving forgiveness of God is used by God to teach us. God wants us to understand how each wrong can hurt others and ourselves. That wisdom should stay with us, but not the shame and guilt. If we daily drag ourselves down into grief, or sorrow, or egocentric anxiety over the *badness* of what we have done, then we can't move ahead and redirect our focus into positive, altruistic actions and thoughts that will enable our *goodness* to grow. God's forgiveness not only renews and uplifts us, but it also frees us to forgive ourselves, to cease being bogged down in guilt and self-hatred.

AS WE FORGIVE THOSE WHO TRESPASS AGAINST US—Forgiving others is usually (but not always) harder than forgiving ourselves. Yet, if we can do this on a regular basis, those being forgiven—openly or silently—can often begin to unconsciously or consciously notice the absence of hatred or rancor or avoidance emanating from us. Instead, they can recognize us as people they can relate to in positive ways . . . people they can trust, or rely on, or talk to. This may or may not lead to friendship, but at least it fosters civil behavior among people in a more positive atmosphere, making it easier to show kindness or just to listen to one another. In addition, if we forgive those who have wronged us, we can begin to have more tolerance and less hatred.

These two petitions in The Lord's Prayer can also help us to acknowledge our weaknesses. "Forgive us our trespasses" reminds us to consider our own wrongdoings *before* we focus on the faults of others. As Jesus put it, "Notice the log in your own eye first." (Mt. 7.3) And then, when we go on to say, "As we forgive those who trespass against us," we should be centered not on forgiving the sins, but forgiving the sinners, acknowledging that neither they *nor* we are perfect, and that all of us are in need of God's mercy and forgiveness. A little bad, a lot of bad; it all goes into a Bad Basket. Moreover, no amount of doing good things can erase the bad things. The only one holding an eraser is God, and God absolves the bad, not because we deserve it, but even though we *don't* deserve it. Through that amazing grace, all of us can be restored.

AND LEAD US NOT INTO TEMPTATION—Does God ever actually *lead* us into temptation? No. God gives us the freedom to act or think as we choose, but does not push us towards temptation. There are many other voices, inside and outside us, that can easily do that job. So, the most important word in this phrase is the word *not*. And this petition is reinforced by the following phrase:

BUT DELIVER US FROM EVIL—We can *often* rely on ourselves, and/or on one or more others, for the strength to move away from evil thoughts, words, or action. But the one we can *always* rely on, our Deliverer and Savior, is God. Although God is always there, the decision to accept or reject that helping hand, to grab it or to shove it away, is up to us. So, for God's forgiveness to work, we have to forgive ourselves. Moreover, as Jesus taught us, (Mt.6.14-15) we need to forgive others as well; for if our hearts and minds are so hard that we do not forgive them, then we are also closing ourselves off from God's forgiveness.

Interestingly, although the first parts of this prayer are very concise, these last two petitions actually say the same thing twice. To paraphrase: "Lead us not into evil, but lead us away from evil." Of course, it's well known that this type of parallel construction is quite common in ancient Hebrew literature, especially in the Psalms, for example: "Lift up your heads, O gates! and be lifted up, O ancient doors!" (Ps.24.7) or "Make me to know your ways, O Lord; teach me your paths." (Ps.25.4). Note also that Jesus continued to use the plural pronouns throughout The Lord's Prayer: Give *us* this day *our* daily bread, and forgive *us our* trespasses as *we* forgive those who trespass against *us*. Lead *us* not into temptation but deliver *us* from evil." How strangely different it would be if singular pronouns were used: "Give *me* this day *my* daily bread, and forgive *me my* trespasses as *I* forgive those who trespass against *me*; and lead *me* not into temptation, but deliver *me* from evil." (See Appendix 4 for other good word choices for *forgive*, *lead*, and *deliver*.)

The Lord's Prayer is very versatile. It can be used as a private prayer in our personal devotions. It can be spoken with a friend or with one or more close family members. It can be used in a Bible study group, or also with fellow worshippers in a chapel, church, or cathedral, with a dozen of others or with thousands, for The Lord's Prayer is a prayer of unity and solidarity, in which God listens to one and all.

This is the end of the Lord's Prayer as it was spoken by Jesus to his followers and written down by two of Jesus' disciples.

Part 2

Matthew's and Luke's versions of The Lord's Prayer

THE LORD'S PRAYER IS recorded twice in the New Testament: once in the Gospel of Matthew 6.5-13 (AD 60 - 70) and once in the Gospel of Luke 11.1-4 (AD 60 - 65), approximately thirty years after the Crucifixion.

MATTHEW states that the prayer is given during the Sermon on the Mount. First, Jesus is talking about how *not* to pray:

> And when you pray, do not be like the hypocrites; for they love to stand and pray in the synagogues and at the street corners, so that they may be seen by others. Truly I tell you, they have received their reward. But whenever you pray, go into your room and shut the door and pray to your Father who is in secret; and your Father who sees in secret will reward you. When you are praying, do not heap up empty phrases as the Gentiles do; for they think they will be heard because of their many words. Do not be like them, for your Father knows what you need before you ask him. Pray then in this way:

> Our Father in heaven, hallowed be your name.
> Your kingdom come.
> Your will be done, on earth as it is in heaven.
> Give us this day our daily bread.
> And forgive us our debts,
> as we also have forgiven our debtors.
> And do not bring us to the time of trial,
> but rescue us from the evil one. (New RSV)

LUKE introduces a shorter version of the prayer in a different way:

> Jesus was praying in a certain place, and after he had finished, one of his disciples said to him, "Lord, teach us to pray, as John [The Baptist] taught his disciples." He said to them, "When you pray, say:
>
> Father, hallowed be your name.
> Your kingdom come.
> Give us each day our daily bread.
> And forgive our sins,
> for we ourselves forgive everyone indebted to us.
> And do not bring us to the time of trial." (New RSV)

— *Part 3* —

The Doxology

Some Christians add one more part at the end of the prayer:

> *For thine is the kingdom, and the power, and the glory, for ever and ever. Amen.*

Though *Amen* is not used in Matthew or Luke at the conclusion of The Lord's Prayer, it is commonly spoken at the end of the doxology. *Amen* is a very old word and has never changed from the ancient Hebrew, to Greek, to Latin, to modern languages. It's used as a strong affirmation of *all* the words in a prayer. Literally, it means "Certainly," or "Truly," or "So be it," or "Make it so."

This concluding petition is called a *doxology*, a liturgical expression of praise [from the Greek "doxa," honor or glory, and "logos," word or speech]. Doxologies have been used for thousands of years and are often found in several Psalms (for ex., 41.13, 72.19, 89.52, 106.48).

Many of them were probably used orally for centuries before finally being written down.

For example, the doxology at the end of the Lord's Prayer is very similar to a passage from the Old Testament *Book of I Chronicles* (29.10-11). These words were written in the 5th century BC, and are ascribed to King David, who lived in the 10th century BC. Some biblical scholars think that The Lord's Prayer doxology (highlighted below in *italics*) may have been borrowed from these verses:

> "Blessed are you, O Lord, the God of our ancestor Israel, *forever and ever.* Thine, O Lord, is the greatness, *and the power, and the glory,* and the victory, and the majesty; for all that is in the heavens and in the earth is thine; *thine is the kingdom*, O Lord, and thou art exalted as head above all." (RSV)

Although the doxology does not appear in most of the early manuscripts of the New Testament, it apparently has been used by Christians since ancient times. For example, in the 1st century, one form of it was used in the *Didacte*, a brief manual of instruction for Christian converts:

> "For thine is the power and the glory forever."

Today, most Protestants use the doxology. Roman Catholics use it in the Mass, but not in the rosary during private prayer.

There are a number of possible reasons for the absence or the presence of the doxology:

1. In ancient times, many pieces of information that people deemed important were passed down orally from one generation to the next, so variations of The Lord's Prayer were bound to occur over the years.
2. Another reason is that in the first few centuries, the early Christians had *many* versions of the New Testament. The Good News spread very fast. Biblical scholars have tracked down over 5,000 ancient Greek manuscripts of the New Testament! Most of the words were the same, but there were some differences, including the doxology phrase. Some had it; some didn't.
3. After 1517, Protestants split from the Roman Catholic Church. Martin Luther translated the New Testament from

Greek into German in 1522, and he used the doxology at the end of the Lord's Prayer. However, in 1526, when he wrote *The Small Catechism*, he did not include the doxology.

In England, new editions of bibles and prayer books were soon available. William Tyndale, who translated the Bible from the original Greek in 1526, used the doxology after The Lord's Prayer in the Gospel of Matthew, as did the *Geneva Bible* of 1560 (used by Shakespeare and the Mayflower Pilgrims) and also *The King James Bible* in 1611. The first Anglican *Book of Common Prayer* (1546) did not have the doxology after the Lord's Prayer. However, Elizabeth I (who reigned from 1558 to 1603) wanted the doxology used to further separate Anglican worship from the Roman Catholic church. The doxology does appear in the 1668 edition of the *BCP*.

By the 20th century, Lutheran children were taught The Lord's Prayer with the doxology at home and in Sunday school. In a number of Lutheran hymnals published in the late 1990s (e.g. the Lutheran *Service Book and Hymnal*), the Lord's Prayer was spoken by the pastor in the communion service, and then the congregation would sing the doxology.

4. Geographical differences occurred as well. In early Christianity, Catholics in the western part of the Roman Empire didn't use the doxology; those in the eastern part did. The western Catholics formed the Roman Catholic Church, and the eastern Catholics formed the Eastern Orthodox Church.

Today, both Roman and Orthodox Catholics use TLP during Mass in the following ways:

ROMAN CATHOLIC:

All: Our Father, who art in heaven, hallowed be thy name;

thy kingdom come, thy will be done on earth as it is
in heaven.

Give us this day our daily bread, and forgive us
our trespasses,

as we forgive those who trespass against us;

and lead us not into temptation, but deliver us from evil.

Priest: Deliver us, Lord, we pray, from every evil, graciously

grant peace in our days, that, by the help of your mercy,

we may be always free from sin and safe from all distress,

as we await the blessed hope and the coming of our Savior, Jesus Christ.

Congregation: For the kingdom, the power and the glory are yours now and for ever.

ORTHODOX:

All: Our Father, who art in heaven, hallowed be thy name;

thy kingdom come; thy will be done on earth as it is in heaven.

Give us this day our daily bread, and forgive us our sins

as we forgive those who sin against us;

and lead us not into temptation, but deliver us from the evil one.

Priest: For thine is the kingdom, and the power, and the glory

of the Father, and of the Son, and of the Holy Spirit,

now and ever and unto the ages of ages.

All: Amen.

Part 4

Ancient Versions of The Lord's Prayer

Aramaic, Greek, and Latin

THE ARAMAIC VERSION

Of course, when Jesus spoke to his people, he used Aramaic, a language akin to Hebrew, with letters that were similar in appearance. There are several different phonetic variants of the Aramaic Lord's Prayer.

Dr. David Mitchell, biblical theologian and author of several books on religion, gives us many insights into Aramaic. Originally, it was a tribal language of Syria, but in the 8th century B.C. the ruler Tiglath-Pileser III decided to use it as the official language of his Assyrian Empire, which covered all the territories from Egypt to India. As Mitchell tells it, from 700 to 200 B.C., Aramaic as a "lingua franca" became "one of the greatest languages in the world."[1] (See Appendix 5 for more details on international languages.)

Aramaic was the native language of Abraham, and Moses taught his people to say, "My father was a wandering Aramean" (Deut. 26.5). It had become the common language of the people in Galilee, including Jesus. He and his disciples also knew Greek, which by then had become widely used throughout the

1. Mitchell, "Lord's Prayer in Aramaic."

Mediterranean world. Aramaic was spoken in the Jewish temples, but Hebrew was used to read the scriptures. So, many of the people in the time of Jesus were trilingual.[2]

Although the language of Aramaic is related to Hebrew, there are several differences. As Mitchell describes it: "Linguistically, Aramaic sits halfway between Hebrew and Arabic, just like Dutch sits halfway between English and German."[3]

There have been several different variants of Aramaic, but only two representative manuscripts of The Lord's Prayer have survived. They are called the Curetonian text and the Synoptic Syriac text. They both have most of the same words used in the Greek text of the Gospels. Today the Aramaic-speaking churches of the East use the Syriac Peshitta. ("Peshitta" means "plain" or "simple".)

So, what were Jesus' exact words? According to Mitchell: "The only way you could be sure of the 100% original text would be if you had been present at the Sermon on the Mount."[4]

There are two different versions of The Lord's Prayer in Aramaic. One of them is the *Peshitta* Aramaic, translated by David Mitchell.[5]

Here is the other version of The Lord's Prayer in *Galilean* Aramaic, the one Jesus used:

2. Google offers some sites where you can *listen* to TLP in Aramaic.
3. Mitchell, "Lord's Prayer in Aramaic."
4. Mitchell, "Lord's Prayer in Aramaic."
5. See his translation at his website: brightmorningstar.org.

The Lord's Prayer—In the Language Jesus Likely Spoke.
(1st century Galilean Aramaic)[6]

ܐܒܘܢ ܕܒܫܡܝܐ
Abwoon d'bashmaya
→ Our Father in heaven

ܢܬܩܕܫ ܫܡܟ
Nethqadash shmakh
→ Halowed be Your Name

ܬܐܬܐ ܡܠܟܘܬܟ
Tethe malkuthakh
→ Your kingdom come

ܢܗܘܐ ܨܒܝܢܟ ܐܝܟܢܐ ܕܒܫܡܝܐ ܐܦ ܒܐܪܥܐ
Nehwe sebyonakh aykano d'bashmaya aph b'ar'a
→ Your will be done on earth as it is in heaven

ܗܒ ܠܢ ܠܚܡܐ ܕܢܘܗܝܢ ܝܘܡܢܐ
Hab lan lakhma d'nawhin yawmana
→ Give us today our daily bread

ܘܫܒܘܩ ܠܢ ܚܘܒܝܢ ܘܚܛܗܝܢ
Washbuq lan ḥubayn w'ḥatahayn
→ Forgive us our debts as we forgive those indebted to us

ܘܠܐ ܬܥܠܢ ܠܢܣܝܘܢܐ
W'la ta'lan l'nesyuna
→ And do not bring us into temptation

ܐܠܐ ܦܨܢ ܡܢ ܒܝܫܐ
Ela patsan min bisha
→ But deliver us from evil

ܐܡܝܢ
Amen
→ Truly, it is so

In the 1st century, there were several dialects of Aramaic. Jesus used his native Galilean dialect. The modern-day Neo-Aramaic is still used, but only by a few people in isolated communities, so it may not last much longer as a spoken language. However, Aramaic is still studied by Biblical scholars. A few of them say that in one dialect of the Aramaic Lord's Prayer, the word "Father" was "Abwoon," a blending of "abba" (father) and "woon" (womb), indicating God as a masculine *and* feminine source of creation! But many

6. From Manokekame, "The Lord's Prayer – In the Language Jesus Likely Spoke," Facebook, Jan. 20, 2026, https://www.facebook.com/abenamagis/posts/the-lords-prayer-in-the-language-jesus-likely-spokegalilean-aramaic-1st-century-/1436664214499187/.

scholars disagree. (It may be tempting to think that this Aramaic word "woon" is related to the English words "womb" or "woman." However, there is not any etymological evidence to support this.)

THE GREEK VERSION

Greek was the language used by Matthew and Luke, as well as the other Gospel and Epistle writers. They wrote in the common (Koine) Greek used by the learned people of the Middle East. In fact, from the 4th century B.C. through the 5th century A.D., Greek was the international language of the Mediterranean countries. This Greek language is still being taught in several universities and seminaries world-wide, and is used by many priests, deacons, pastors, monks, and lay people to help them understand and interpret the New Testament. (You'll notice that the word order is usually different in Greek.) The chart below gives the pronunciation, the Greek word, and the translation into English:

Pater	Πάτερ	Father
Hemon	ἡμῶν	of us
ho	ὁ	who [is]
en	ἐν	in
tois	τοῖς	the
ouranois	οὐρανοῖς	Heavens
Hagiastheto.	Ἁγιασθήτω.	hallowed be
To	τὸ	The
onoma	ὄνομά	Name
sou	σου	of you
eltheto	ἐλθέτω	come
he	ἡ	the
basilica	βασιλεία	kingdom
sou	σου	of you

genetheto	γενηθήτω	be done
to	τὸ	the
thelma	θέλημά	will
sou	σου	of you
hos	ὡς	as
en	ἐν	in
ourano	οὐρανῷ	heaven
kai	καὶ	[so] also
epi	ἐπὶ	upon
get	γῆς	earth
ton	τὸν	the
arton	ἄρτον	Bread
hemon	ἡμῶν	of us
epiousion	ἐπιούσιον	daily
dos	δὸς	grant
hemin	ἡμῖν	us
semeron	σήμερον	today
kai	καὶ	and
aphes	ἄφες	forgive
hemin	ἡμῖν	us
ta	τὰ	the
opheilemata	ὀφειλήματα	debts
hemon	ἡμῶν	of us
hos	ὡς	as
kai	καὶ	also
hemeis	ἡμεῖς	we
aphekame	ἀφήκαμεν	forgive

tois	τοῖς	the
opheiletais	ὀφειλέταις	debtors
hemon	ἡμῶν	of us

kai	καὶ	and
me	μὴ	not
eisenegkes	εἰσενέγκῃς	lead
hemes	ἡμᾶς	us
his	εἰς	into
peirasmon	πειρασμόν	temptation
alla	ἀλλὰ	but
rhysai	ῥῦσαι	deliver
hemas	ἡμᾶς	us
apo	ἀπὸ	from
ponerou	πονηροῦ	evil

THE LATIN VERSION

Despite frequent persecution of believers, Christianity rapidly spread through the Roman Empire in the 1st century. Eventually, in 313 AD, Emperor Constantine legalized the religion and supported its activities; during one of his councils, the Nicene Creed was formed.

Although the political supremacy of Rome fell in the 4th century, the linguistic power of Latin continued. It was the "lingua franca" in Europe and the Middle East until the late 16th century, used by rulers, scholars, traders, and clerics.

Although a number of Latin biblical manuscripts had come into existence by the 4th century (such as *Vetus Latina,* "the Ancient Latins") it was Pope Damasus I who commissioned St. Jerome to translated the Bible into Latin in 382. This version became known as the *version vulgata* (that is "the commonly used translation") or simply the Vulgate. This is still the standard Latin Bible for the Roman Catholic Church. Though some vernacular versions were used, the Latin words were very familiar to worshippers for centuries. But then in 1963, Pope Paul VI convened a special council, and after this, the use of the vernacular became allowed at Mass. Most American Roman Catholic Churches now use English. For accuracy in the Latin version of TLP below, I used as many cognates as possible (words with a common origin).

Below is the Latin version with the English translation in italics:

Pater noster, qui es in cœlis, sanctificetum nomen tuum:
Father our who is in heaven, sanctified (be) name your

Adventiat regnum tuum; fiat voluntas tua, sicut in cœlo, et in terra.
Come realm your; done volition your, as in heaven, so on earth

Panem nostrum quotidianum da nobis hodie:
Bread our of every day give us today.

Et dimitte nobis debita nostra et nos dimittius debitoribus nostris:
And dismiss us debs our as we dismiss debtors our

et ne nos inductas in tentationem: sed libera nos a malo.
And not us induce into temptation but liberate us from malice

The first two words of this prayer, "Pater noster" have been used as the name of this prayer for two thousand years. Many English-speaking Catholics still refer to it as the "Our Father." In fact, the prayer was not called "The Lord's Prayer" until the Protestant Reformation of the 16th century. [For more on non-Latin Bibles, see Appendix 6.]

Part 5

The English Versions of The Lord's Prayer

HISTORICALLY, THE ENGLISH VERSIONS of this prayer changed as the English language changed over the centuries, beginning with the Old English that the Anglo-Saxons used a thousand years ago.

(I translated this prayer in 1974 and created the chart below.)

AD 995 OLD ENGLISH

Several OE translations of TLP were made from Greek & Latin.

Fæder ure	Father our
þu þe eart on heofonum,	thou that art in heaven
si þin nama gehalgod.	be thine name hallowed.
Tobecume þin rice.	Come thy kingdom.
Gewurþe ðin willa on eorðan.	Be honored (Be worthy) thine will on earth
swa swa on heofonum.	just as in heaven

Urne gedæghwamlican hlaf syle us todæg.	our daily bread (loaf) give us today.
And forgyf us ure gyltas swa swa	And forgive us our guilts just as
forgyfað urum gyltendum.	we forgive against us those guilty.
And ne gelæd þu us on costnunge,	And not lead thou us into temptation (trials)
ac alys us of yfele.	but loosen us (free us) of evil.
Soþlice.	Truth-like (Truly, Amen).

1389 MIDDLE ENGLISH

Here we see *many* changes in words and syntax.

John Wycliffe (c. 1328-1384) translated the Bible into Middle English from the Latin Vulgate because he wanted to make it available to the common people. He said the papal claims of temporal power had no biblical foundation. He argued that Christian beliefs and practices should be based on the scriptures alone; and "he came to emphasize the saving power of Christ rather than the priestly mediation . . . of the organized church." (Stephenson & Lyon, *Mediaeval History*, 510) Wycliffe not only spoke out against corruption in the church, but also against serfdom and warfare. Then, in the early 1400s, the church posthumously proclaimed him a heretic, burned his books, disinterred him, and burned his body. (For more info, see Appendix 6)

Oure fadir.
That art in hevenes
Halwid be thi name
Thi kingdom come to
Be thi wille don
On erthe as in hevenes
Give to us this day our bred [ovir other substances]
And forgive us our debts
As we forgiven our detours
And lede us not to temptation
But deliver us from yvel. Amen

1526 EARLY MODERN ENGLISH

William Tyndale (1792-1536) translated the TLP from the Greek, and here he added a doxology. His Bible was the first one to be published from a printing press. Tyndale admired Erasmus and Martin Luther, who advocated church reforms. He was so criticized by Roman Catholics in England he fled to Europe. In 1535 he was imprisoned, and the following year was strangled and burned at the stake for heresy. Even so, Tyndale's vernacular version soon became widely used.[1]

> O oure father which arte in heven,
> halowed be thy name;
> let thy kingdom come;
> thy wyll be fulfilled
> as well in erth as hit ys in heven;
> geve vs this daye oure dayly breade;
> and forgeve vs oure treaspases,
> even as we forgeve them which treaspas vs;
> leede vs not into temptacion,
> but delyvre vs from yvell.
> For thyne is the kingdom and the power,[4]
> and the glorye for ever.
> Amen.

1549 From the first Anglican *Book of Common Prayer*

> Our father, whyche art in heaven,
> halowed be thy name.
> Thy Kyngdome come.
> Thy wyll be doen in yearth,
> as it is in heaven.

1. Some of the biographical facts about Wycliff and Tyndale, as well as the wording of the 1549 edition of the BCP, were gleaned from Wikipedia, "William Tyndale," Wikipedia, "John Wycliffe," and from the *Funk & Wagnalls New Encyclopedia*, vol. 28, p. 28 and vol. 26, p. 130.

Geve us this daye our dayly breade.
And forgeve us our trespaces,
as wee forgeve them that trespasse agaynst us.
And leade us not into temptacion.
But deliver us from evill. Amen.

1611 *King James Version.*

Translated from the Greek by a group of 54 scholars, who apparently depended heavily on Tyndale's translation. According to one estimate, 83% of the New Testament and 76% of the Old Testament was based on Tyndale's work.[2]

Our father which art in heauen,
hallowed be thy name
Thy kingdome come.
Thy will be done,
in earth, as it is in heauen.
Giue vs this day our daily bread.
And forgiue vs our debts,
as we forgiue our debters.
And lead vs not into temptation,
but deliuer vs from euill:
For thine is the kingdome, and the power,
and the glory, for euer.
Amen.

1759 *Ordo administrandi sacramenta*

"Order for Administring the Sacraments," composed by Bishop Richard Challoner. [Anglican version, from *wikipedia.org.*]

Our Father who art in heaven,
hallowed be thy name.

2. Wikipedia, "King James Version."

Thy kingdom come.
Thy will be done
on earth as it is in heaven.
Give us this day our daily bread,
and forgive us our trespasses,
as we forgive them that trespass against us,
and lead us not into temptation,
but deliver us from evil. Amen
[By 1772, the *Book of Common Prayer* had added the doxology.]

1928 MODERN ENGLISH.

The Anglican *Book of Common Prayer* (similar to the 2016 Episcopal BCP, q.v.)

Our Father, who art in heaven,
Hallowed be thy Name.
Thy kingdom come.
Thy will be done,
On earth as it is in heaven.
Give us this day our daily bread.
And forgive us our trespasses,
As we forgive those who trespass against us.
And lead us not into temptation,
But deliver us from evil.
For thine is the kingdom, and the power,
and the glory, for ever and ever.
Amen.

Since the early 20th century, the above version has been, and still is, very commonly used by Protestants.

However, in the late 20th century, a newer version has appeared beside it. For example:

1970

The more recent Lutheran and Episcopal Versions are very similar.

Our Father in heaven,
hallowed be your name,
your kingdom come,
your will be done,
on earth as in heaven.
Give us today our daily bread.
Forgive us our sins
as we forgive those who sin against us.
Save us from the time of trial
and deliver us from evil.
For the kingdom, the power, and the glory
are yours now and for ever. Amen.

As we have seen, the words and pronunciation of our English language have changed significantly through the years, from Old English (450-1100) to Middle English (1100-1450) then to Early Modern English (1450-1750) and next into Modern English (1750-present).

There were also many changes in the ancient languages of Aramaic, Greek, and Latin. However, the *meaning* of the words in The Lord's Prayer has remained consistent for two thousand years!

— Part 6 —

"Trespasses" or "Debts." Which one do you use?

THERE ARE TWO WORDS in the Lord's Prayer (*trespass* and *trespasses*) which, through the years, have been translated in a number of different ways:

According to Greek lexicons, the original words in ancient Koine Greek (which Matthew and Luke used) translate as *debts* and *debtors*, but can *also* be translated as *delinquencies, offenses, faults, wrong-doings* or *sins*. The other viable synonym, *trespassses*, did not come to be commonly used until the 16th century. A number of modern languages use some form of *debt* and *debtors*:

Greek, debts (ὀφειλήματα) and debtors (ὀφειλέταις)

Latin: debita, debitoribi

Italian: debiti, debitori

Spanish: deudas, deudores

In German: *Schuld, Schuldigern* can be translated as "debt" and debtors," but also as "sin, sinners; fault, faulty ones, offense, offenders; guilt, guilty ones."

In French, we have:

Pardonne-nous nos *offenses,*

comme nous pardonnons aussi à ceux qui nous ont *offensés.*

(That is: "Pardon us our *offenses* as we pardon also those who have *offended* us.")

To get a *complete* comparison of word choices, we would have to consult *all* the languages in the world into which the New Testament has been translated. So far, that would be about 1600 languages. Today, there are over 7000 different languages in the world, so we still have quite a way to go yet.

English translations, for the past 1000 years, have used different word choices:

In 10th century Old English, the people used *gyltas,* the origin of our word "guilts," (but this word, back then, was also used for "debts.")

In 1386, in Middle English, John Wycliffe used *dettis, dettours*

In 1526, William Tyndale was the first to use *treaspases. trespas.*

(These are Middle English words, not used before the 14th century.)

In 1611, in Early Modern English, the *King James Bible* again used *debts, debtors,* as did some Modern English Bibles in the 20th century:

1941 *The Revised Standard Version,*

1989 *The New Revised Standard Version,*

1982 *The New Testament Revised Berkeley Version* (the *Gideon Bible* in hotels).

In 1961 *The New English Bible—New Testament* (Oxford & Cambridge) used the phrases "the *wrong* we have done . . . those who have *wronged* us."

In 1966 *The Good News Bible* used "the *wrongs* we have done. . . the *wrongs* that others have done to us"

In 1971 *The Book* (a special edition of *The Living Bible*) has "and forgive us our *sins* . . . those who have *sinned* against us."

In 1991 the "easy-to-read" *Contemporary English Version* similarly used "Forgive us for doing *wrong*, as we forgive others."

> Today, the most common choices are *debts* or *trespasses*.
>
> Presbyterians and other Reformed churches usually use *debts*.
>
> Roman Catholics, Episcopalians, Lutheran, and Methodists usually use *trespasses*.

It is important to realize that *all* the versions carry the meaning and intention of Jesus' words. Usually, we are most comfortable using the words we have memorized, the ones that we have been used to saying since we were younger.

The issue is complicated by the fact that in Modern English, the words *debt* is often used in the context of owing someone money, goods, services, or favors. Likewise, our word *trespass* commonly means to go onto someone's property without permission. It should be recognized, however, that historically *both* of those words can have the same negative synonyms: sin, wrong, wrongdoing, offense, guilt, transgression, wickedness, iniquity, fault, error, evil, and misdeed. So, the important thing is not the specific *sounds* that are produced in our voices, but the general *intentions* that are produced in our hearts and minds.

Moreover, sometimes, as the old saying goes, "Variety is the spice of life." So, occasionally using the term "wrongs" or "sins" might give us a chance to stop and think about what we're saying and to find different ways of understanding this part of The Lord's Prayer.

Sometimes God must be smiling at us, as when we make such a fuss in trying to decide exactly which words to choose, when the really important thing is that God has the power to forgive us if we do bad things, and we have the power (with God's help) to forgive others.

Part 7

Other Versions of The Lord's Prayer

HERE ARE A FEW other variations of the Lord's Prayer which can also give us pause for reflection:

For the past five hundred years, even deists have used The Lord's Prayer.

In 1768, Benjamin Franklin wrote his version (at a time when Early Modern English was changing into Modern English):

> Heavenly Father,
> May all revere thee,
> And become thy dutiful Children and faithful Subjects.
> May thy Laws be obeyed on Earth as perfectly as they are in Heaven.
> Provide for us this Day as thou has* hitherto daily done.
> Forgive us our Trespasses, and enable us likewise to forgive those that offend us.
> Keep us out of Temptation, and deliver us from Evil.

*(Apparently, Ben forgot to put in the "t" for the word "hast," and, as far as I know, no one has ever corrected this.)

In 1830, *The Book of Mormon* was written down by Joseph Smith. It includes The Lord's Prayer (recorded in 3 Nephi 13.9-13). Since it reflected the beliefs that "God's kingdom was already inaugurated" and that "the Risen Lord" was already the "Bread of Life," two petitions in the prayer were omitted.[1]

> Our Father who art in heaven, hallowed be thy name. [. . . .]
> Thy will be done on earth as it is in heaven. [. . . .]
> And forgive us our debts as we forgive our debtors
> And lead us not into temptation, but deliver us from evil.
> For thine is the kingdom, and the power, and the glory, forever. Amen.

1997 The Lord's Prayer: Maori & Polynesia [2]

> Eternal Spirit,
> Earth-maker, Pain-bearer, Life-giver,
> Source of all that is and that shall be,
> Father and Mother of us all,
> Loving God, in whom is heaven:
> The hallowing of your name echo through the universe!
> The way of your justice be followed by the peoples of the world!
> Your heavenly will be done by all created beings!
> Your commonwealth of peace and freedom
> sustain our hope and come on earth.
> With the bread we need for today, feed us.
> In the hurts we absorb from one another, forgive us.
> In times of temptation and test, strengthen us.
> From trial too great to endure, spare us.
> From the grip of all that is evil, free us.
> For you reign in the glory of the power that is love,
> now and forever. Amen.

1. For a full commentary on this version of the prayer, see Scripture Central, "Why is the Lord's Prayer Different in 3 Nephi?"

2. From the *New Zealand Book of Prayer of the Anglican Church.*

The poem below, based on the words in The Lord's Prayer, is a psalm of praise and thanksgiving for what God has already done for us and continues to do for us each day:

Each day, our heavenly Father,
your name remains sacred to us.
Each day, since the beginning of time,
    your heavenly rule and your will
    have been coming into being here on earth.
Each day, you provide us with our basic needs
    (though sometimes we misuse them).
Each day, you forgive us our wrongdoings.
Each day, you give us the merciful power of love
    to forgive others when they do us wrong.
Each day, you lead us and direct us awa from
    evil deeds, evil words, and evil thoughts
    (though sometimes we do not follow).
Each day, we strive to remember that you possess
    the ultimate and eternal dominion, power, and glory.
Each day, for all these things, we thank you.

Afterword

WORDS. THEY HELP US communicate with others and with ourselves. They also help us to think and to act. The words of The Lord's Prayer exist in many different versions and are used every day by people all over the world. The particular version that we first learn as children, or as adults, is usually the one with which we are most comfortable. It's like an old friend. We know it by heart. We can easily recite it at any time at any place. It also feels really good to say the words at religious gatherings, when we are with other people who are saying exactly the same words.

However, there is one problem. Even though we love the prayer, we know the words so well that our minds can sometimes wander while reciting them. We begin to think of other things in the past, present, or future.

That's why, once in a while, it may be good for us to use a different version of The Lord's Prayer, either an older one or a modern one. The change in wording might not only sharpen our focus, but also broaden our understanding of what Jesus was teaching us. It might well give our minds, and hearts, and spirits something new to dwell on, long after the words have been spoken.

We're very fortunate, in a way. Many authors, after they die, "live on" through their words that have been written down. Jesus, the author of The Lord's Prayer, really does live on. He taught us the prayer, and now God—through Jesus and the Father and the Holy Spirit—listens to us every time we say this prayer. God also speaks to us through this prayer, because each recitation of it is an opportunity to realize and learn about God's holiness, God's power, God's will, God's provisions, God's forgiveness, and God's guidance. What a prayer! What a wonder-full, joy-full, peace-full gift of love! May it continue to be so, for today, for tomorrow, for ever and ever. Amen. Thank you, God.

— *Appendix 1* —

God the Creator

MANY OF THE WORLD's believers regard God as the Creator. Some do not. (In fact, some people don't accept any higher power, even one that gives them their own powers of brain and body.) However, for those who do, this psalm (which I wrote a few years ago) speaks of the extent of God's power:

O God, Ruler of the Universe,
Creator of every good thing and every good thought,
the world you have given us is filled with so much
goodness and beauty and harmony and light
that our hearts and minds and senses are filled to overflowing
with wonder, and joy, and peace.

Every living thing in the universe owes its existence to you:
Every animal that runs, walks, crawls, hops, swims, or flies;
Every breath they take, every beat their hearts make
is possible because of you.

Every plant that sprouts and expands in its greenness,
Every flower that blossoms into
beautiful shapes and bountiful colors can grow
because of the gift of life you have bestowed upon it.

Every stone and boulder on hill, plain, or mountain,
Every grain of sand on every beach by pond, lake, or ocean
was formed from your power.

Every cloud, every glowing ray of sunshine or flash of light,
Every sunrise and sunset, every rainbow,
Every breeze or gale or breath of wind,
Every drop of rain or flake of snow
surrounds us, or passes by us, or rests upon us,
having been sent from above
by you, God, the Giver of all good things.

You fill our eyes with splendid sights
of sparkling streams or snow-covered trees beside us,
the aerial ballets of birds above us,
the glorious green of grass and moss and meadows
beneath us.

You fill our ears with musical sounds,
from crickets, frogs, and robins,
from the wondrous whispers of winds
through the branches of pines,
from the pleasing patterns of water-voices
flowing out from brooks, rapids, and waterfalls.

You fill our nostrils with the fragrance of flowers,
and the fresh salty air of the sea,
and the pungent fullness of forested pathways.

The multiplicity of your blessings is so abundant
that sometimes we scarcely can take it in.

Your kingdom does come on earth as it is in heaven.
You are our Maker, our Parent, our Provider,
our Source of Perfect Peace.
Keep us mindful of your daily gifts.
Keep us grateful for your ever-present goodness.

Appendix 2

God Names

There are thousands of names for gods.
The one you use depends on
your religion,
your language,
and your traditional background.

How many names for God in the Holy Bible?
Sone websites list hundreds.
Which name does God prefer?

The best answer I've seen was in
the Old Testament Book of Exodus (3.14).
When Moses asked God what name should be used,
God said, "I am who I am."

— *Appendix 3* —

Heaven on Earth

Can there really be a heaven on earth? Are we asking for the impossible? Can God's kingdom come and his will be done on earth just as it is in heaven?

Sometimes we get discouraged because its often difficult, or seemingly impossible, for us to accept the idea of "heaven on earth" as a logical reality . . . especially when we experience so much negativity in our lives:

The destruction from wars laying waste to fields, homes, schools, hospitals, stores, offices, churches, temples, and synagogues. So much death—not only of militants, but of civilian men, women, and children.

The ever-present environmental damages to our air, land, and water. The human damage caused by greed, jealousy, anger, and abuse—mental and physical—that rips apart the stability of countries, cities, towns, neighborhoods, and families. The debilitating damage from storms, floods, heat waves, and plagues.

The pain of mental and physical health problems: dementia, depression, anxiety, injuries, sickness, and organ failures.

The list goes on and on. So, where and when does God's kingdom come? Where and when can his will be done? So, what good can prayer do?

Praying daily for heaven on earth can make us more conscious of the good around us—enabling us to focus and better see and hear and feel the positive things that exists amongst all the negative things. It is there. God is there.

An old tune from the 60s goes, "All we saying is give peace a chance."[1]

In other words: Let the goodness break through the badness. Listen for it. Look for it. Live for it.

"Thy kingdom come. Thy will be done."

1. Wikipedia, "Give Peace a Chance." This was John Lennon's spontaneous response on June 1, 1969, when a Montreal reporter asked him what he wanted to achieve by protesting the Vietnam War.

Appendix 4

Forgive, *Lead*, and *Deliver*

Some additional word choices for *forgive*, *lead*, and *deliver*, as used in the original Greek and Latin texts:

In Greek—*forgive* is written as ἄφες [aphes] which means *remit* or, literally, *send away*.

In Latin—the version uses the word *dimitte*, which means *send in a different direction*.

In Greek—the word for *lead* is εἰσενέγκῃς [eisenegkes] translates as *carry* or *bring*. The word *carry* works well here because it has the connotation of being completely dependent on God to lead us away from temptation

In Latin—the word *inducas* (root of *induce* in English) originally meant *pull* or *draw over*.

In Greek—the word for *deliver* is written as ῥῦσαι [rusai], a very strong word meaning *rescue*.

In Latin—the verb for this was *libera*, which of course means *free*. It's another strong word which is asking God to *liberate* us from evil.

(N.B. The purpose of mentioning these words is not to have them replace the words we already use, but only to shed some extra light on the passages.)

Appendix 5

Universal Languages

THE USE OF A *lingua franca* made intercommunication much easier among people from different countries and different language groups. For example, because St. Paul and St. Peter were fluent in Greek, they could connect with speakers of many other Mediterranean language communities and more easily promulgate their ideas and beliefs. From ancient times to the present, the prominence of different universal languages changed as follows:

Aramaic:	8th to the 3rd century B.C.
Greek:	early 4th century B.C. to the 5th century A.D.
Latin:	late 5th century to the late 16th century
French:	17th century to the mid-20th century
English:	mid-20th century to the present

— *Appendix 6* —

Non-Latin Bibles

THE ROMAN CATHOLIC BIBLE, the Latin Vulgate version, was the one used in Western European churches for centuries. However, by the late 1300s, some religious scholars believed the Bible should be written in the common language of the people. These vernacular English versions (as well as Martin Luther's German Bible), though not readily accepted by the Vatican, were often used by the general populace, especially since the printing press made books more affordable, and the Protestant Reformation made churches independent of the Vatican.

Appendix 7

The Universality of The Lord's Prayer

2000 YEARS AGO, JESUS of Nazareth was a spiritual teacher. His followers often called him "rabbi," the Hebrew word for teacher. When they asked him to teach them how to pray, he gave them The Lord's Prayer. What I didn't realize until recently is that its basic concepts are now considered to be very important to almost all of the eight billion people in our world.

This prayer itself is used by all Christians. Moreover, each one of the teachings within the prayer is emphasized by the people in all non-Christian religions as well, for example Islam, Hinduism, Buddhism, Judaism, Islam, and many others. Studying some of their different practices—such as deep meditation and the frequency of communal prayer—can help us enhance our own ways of worship.

In addition, all of the basic ideas in The Lord's Prayer are important to the millions of indigenous people throughout the world. They include the aboriginal people of Australia, the natives of North and South America, and the indigenous people of Asia and Africa. For example, the Tribal Prayer of the Omaha people ("Wakonda tay-too wa-pa-tee a-ton-hay"—"Great Spirit, poor and needy here one stands, and I am the one."). Compare this to Psalm

70: "'God is great! But I am poor and needy; hasten to help me, O God." (vs. 4-5. RSV)

All of these traditional communities have a strong belief in a higher power. They speak over 4000 different languages, and there are thousands of names for their Creator, usually translated as the Great Spirit or the Sacred Spirit. Most of us know about Mother Nature or Mother Earth. For these people, *all* of nature is holy: hills, plants, rocks, and bodies of water. All animals are considered to be their brothers and sisters. The American naturalist John Muir, who understood the Native Americans' closeness to nature, once said, "When one tugs at a single thing in nature, he finds it attached to the rest of the world."[1]

There are three basic ideas contained in The Lord's Prayer:

1. The existence of a higher power: "Our Father"
2. The need for physical and mental well-being:
   - acknowledging our need for "daily bread" (such as good food,
   - a good home, good air, land, and water)
   - admitting our "trespasses" (a.k.a. our shortcomings or wrongdoings)
   - forgiving those who "trespass against us," (and, thereby, avoiding an unhealthy over-concern with the misdeeds of others)
3. The need for avoiding "evil" in thoughts, words, and actions.

Except for the first idea, even atheists and agnostics (who make up about seven percent of the world's population) could accept the logic for the second and third ideas. (Atheists reject any possibility for the existence of a god; agnostics say there may be a god, but we have no way of knowing for sure.)

1. Woodley, *Becoming Rooted*, 39.

There are several differences from one belief system to another. However, as humans, it's important for us to remember how much we have in common. Maya Angelou, in her poem "Human Family," tells it this way: "We are more alike, my friends, than we are unalike."[2] Therefore, it seems that people—be they believers, doubters, or deniers—can find benefit from the basic concepts in The Lord's Prayer

There is an old man in our neighborhood who sometimes speaks using traditional and Christian expressions. Every morning before breakfast, he goes outdoors for about an hour or so to feed the furred and feathered animals. "Good morning, all my friends who walk, hop, fly, swim, or crawl. I give my good greetings to all good spirits everywhere: of the land, of the water, and of the air. Let there be peace." (Christians also have good spirits; they usually call them angels.) He then greets the larger beings: "Good morning, Mother Earth, Father Sky" and (whether immediately visible or not) Father Sun, and Mother Moon."

Then he recites aloud his favorite prayer:

Out Father, who art in heaven,
Hallowed be thy name.
Thy kingdom come,
Thy will be done
On earth as it is in heaven.
Give us this day our daily bread,
And forgive us our trespasses,
As we forgive those who trespass against us.
And lead us not into temptation,
But deliver us from evil.
For thine is the kingdom,
And the power, and the glory,
For ever and ever. Amen

2. Angelou, *I Shall Not Be Moved*, 5.

Bibliography

The Analytical Greek Lexicon. New York: Harper & Brothers, 1959.

Angellou, Maya. *I Shall Not Be Moved*. New York: Bantam, 1991.

The Book (a special edition of The Living Bible). Wheaton, IL: Tyndale House Publishers, 1984.

The Book of Common Prayer. (Episcopal). New York: Church Publishing Incorporated, 2016.

The Book of Common Worship. (Presbyterian) 2nd edition, 2015.

The Book of Mormon. Salt Lake City, UT: The Church of Jesus Christ of Latter-day Saints, 1987.

Bram, Leon L., et al. *Funk & Wagnalls New Encyclopedia*. New York: Funk & Wagnalls, Inc. 1983.

Good News Bible. New York: Thomas Nelson Publishers, 1976.

The Holy Bible, King James Version. Cleveland, OH: The World Publishing Company. (The text conforms with the edition of 1611.)

The Holy Bible, New Revised Standard Version. Nashville, TN: Abingdon Press, 1989.

Jordan, Michael. *Encyclopedia of Gods*. New York: Facts On File, 1993.

Luther, Martin. *The Small Catechism*, 1529. Minneapolis, MN: Augsburg Publishing House, published in English in 1979.

Lutheran Book of Worship. Minnesota, MN: Augsburg Publishing House, 1978.

The Lutheran Hymnal. St. Louis, MO: Concordia Publishing House, 1941.

Lutheran Worship. St. Louis, MO: Concordia Publishing House, 1987.

Mitchell, David. "The Lord's Prayer in Aramaic." Bright Morning Star. https://brightmorningstar.org/lords-prayer-in-aramaic/.

Moore, Samuel and Thomas A. Knott. *The Elements of Old English*, 10th ed. Ann Arbor, MI: 1969.

Nestle, Ederhard and Kurt Aland, editors. *Novum Testamentum Graece* (Ancient Greek edition), 1904.

The New English Bible, New Testament. Oxford University Press, 1961.

The Roman Missal. Published by the osvcatholicbookstores.com. 2010.

Scripture Central. "Why Is the Lord's Prayer Different in 3 Nephi?" Aug. 21, 2019. https://scripturecentral.org/knowhy/why-is-the-lords-prayer-different-in-3-nephi.

Seltz, Gregory. "Pray, Praise, and Give Thanks," a sermon on the spiritual powers of The Lord's Prayer doxology, broadcast on The Lutheran Hour, 1/5/14.

Service Book and Hymnal of the LCA. Minnesota, MO: Augsburg Publishing House, 1958.

Stephenson, Carl and Bryce Lyon. *Medial History.* New York: Harper & Row, 1962.

The United Methodist Hymnal. Nashville, TN: The United Methodist Publishing House, 1989.

Wangelin, Bill. "How Does the Lord's Prayer End?" Posted on Our Savior Lutheran Church and School's website: oursaviorlansing.org. 9/9/21.

Wikipedia. "Give Peace a Chance." Wikimedia Foundation, last updated Mar. 10, 2026. https://en.wikipedia.org/wiki/Give_Peace_a_Chance.

———. "History of the Lord's Prayer in English." Wikimedia Foundation, last updated Feb. 18, 2026. https://en.wikipedia.org/wiki/History_of_the_Lord%27s_Prayer_in_English.

———. "John Wycliffe." Wikimedia Foundation, last updated Mar. 14, 2026. https://en.wikipedia.org/wiki/John_Wycliffe.

———. "King James Version." Wikimedia Foundation, last updated Mar. 15, 2026. https://en.wikipedia.org/wiki/King_James_Version.

———. "William Tyndale." Wikimedia Foundation, last updated Mar. 10, 2026. https://en.wikipedia.org/wiki/William_Tyndale.

Woodley, Randy. *Becoming Rooted: One Hundred Days of Reconnecting with Sacred Earth.* Minneapolist: Broadleaf, 2022.

www.ingramcontent.com/pod-product-compliance
Lightning Source LLC
LaVergne TN
LVHW010543100826
845148LV00013B/2582

* 9 7 9 8 3 8 5 2 7 3 6 6 9 *